# VODKA MADE
# ME DO IT

# VODKA MADE ME DO IT

## 60 VIBRANT AND VERSATILE VODKA COCKTAILS

COLLEEN GRAHAM
ILLUSTRATED BY RUBY TAYLOR

HarperCollins*Publishers*

HarperCollins*Publishers*
1 London Bridge Street
London SE1 9GF

www.harpercollins.co.uk

HarperCollins*Publishers*
1st Floor, Watermarque Building,
Ringsend Road
Dublin 4, Ireland

First published by HarperCollins*Publishers* in 2022

1 3 5 7 9 10 8 6 4 2

Text by Colleen Graham
Illustrated by Ruby Taylor
Cover and interior design by Gareth Butterworth

A catalogue record for this book is available from the British Library

ISBN 978-0-00-853037-2

Printed and bound in Latvia

**MIX**
**Paper from**
**responsible sources**
FSC
www.fsc.org
**FSC™ C007454**

# CONTENTS

# INTRODUCTION

The most popular spirit in the world, it's easy to discount vodka as the flavourless, odourless drink it's so often described as. While to some extent that's a fair assessment, the last few decades have proved that vodka is anything but boring. Vodka is continually adapting to market trends and it is now the most mixable distilled spirit you'll find, which is why it makes the ideal base for cocktails.

While vodka is often seen as a spirit used primarily for its alcoholic buzz, it's not just water with a kick. That may be true for some vodkas, but if you take the time to taste enough brands you'll discover subtle nuances. Some have a delicate floral bouquet, those made from corn or wheat may have an underlying sweetness, rye vodkas may be a bit spicy, and potato vodkas are almost buttery. Vodka can be medicinal or have a silky or oily texture. With all of these tasting notes, however, smoothness has long been the measure of good vodka. Today's vodka market doesn't relegate that desired aspect to the top-shelf brands, either. You can find some excellent budget-friendly options that are just as smooth as any high-priced vodka.

All of that makes now a great time to reintroduce yourself to vodka, and cocktails are an excellent way to do this. Within this book you'll find tried-and-tested recipes as well as fun twists on the world's best-known cocktails (not all of which were originally intended for vodka), as well as several classic drinks. My intention is to extend the perception of what's possible with this spirit and encourage everyone to explore its fascinating possibilities.

One of the best ways for this is through homemade infusions, and you'll find plenty of ideas for adding flavour to your favourite vodka on page 20. Sure, you can buy citrus or vanilla vodka off the shelf, but there's a certain satisfaction to making even these common variations at home because you can control every ingredient and develop the flavours to perfectly match your taste. Some of these varieties are made by just a few companies and are tricky to find, while others are obtainable only through a DIY project. The majority of these drinks will also work with straight vodka or another infusion, so mix and match to your heart's content.

Although this is really just a beginner's guide to mixing cocktails, I also hope to teach you a few tricks to creating better drinks – small tips like using fresh produce, homemade mixers, clean ice, and some suggestions for a few basic tools and techniques that will improve every drink you make. Most importantly, any cocktail should be adapted to suit your personal taste. Add more citrus or sweetener, cut back on the soda, pour an extra shot of vodka ... whatever you do, I won't be offended. After all, you're drinking it!

# WHAT IS VODKA?

In the lexicon of distilled spirits, vodka is an open book that's interpreted by each distiller. Technically, vodka is clear spirit distilled from any starchy or sugary ingredient. Traditionally, this was a grain such as rye or wheat, potatoes, or sugar beet molasses. Modern vodkas are distilled from corn, rice, grapes or other fruits, sorghum, soya beans, or even just straight sugar.

Vodka's possibilities can reach the boundaries of other spirits. Molasses and sugar vodkas can have a rum-like taste, grain vodkas are similar to unaged whisky and fruit-based vodkas are not entirely different from brandy except they don't spend time in a barrel. Vodka really is the catch-all distilled spirit. As long as it's clear and neutrally flavoured, everything that doesn't conveniently fit into another category or adhere to certain standards often gets classified as vodka.

## THE ORIGINS OF VODKA

The exact birth of vodka is unclear and subject to conflicting narratives. Beyond oral traditions and lost written records, any history that pertains to intoxicating beverages (whether spirits or cocktails) should take the nature of the beast into account.

The first distilled spirits date back to ancient times. While no hard evidence exists, someone somewhere in the world once had the thought of introducing fermented beer or wine to intense heat and capturing the vapours to create a more potent beverage. It may even have happened simultaneously in multiple regions. By the twelfth century, Europeans were refining the technique of creating agua ardens ('burning water') and aqua vitae ('water of life'). That knowledge was passed along trade routes to Europe's Baltic region, where grains like rye and wheat were bountiful, inexpensive commodities.

Both Poland and Russia claim to be the birthplace of vodka, and each nation might have learned about distillation through interactions with Italians during the twelfth and thirteenth centuries. There may have been a Mongolian influence from the other side of Russia as well. The first written account of wódka was in a 1405 Polish court document, while in Russia, voda (вода – translated to 'little water') made its initial print appearance in the early 1500s.

By the sixteenth century, vodka was the national drink of both Russia and Poland. It was cheap to make from whatever grains were available, so, for instance, potato vodka emerged in Poland. In the Russian Empire, the government quickly figured out that stronger alcohol led to higher taxes, so vodka was promoted to the people over lighter beers and wines (at times, even forced on peasants who wished to abstain) and became one of the largest revenue sources until the world wars (both Tsar

Nicholas II and Vladimir Lenin were prohibitionists). Its popularity came back a bit in the mid-twentieth century, but (while not banned) vodka was discouraged by Mikhail Gorbachev.

During this troubled time, several Russian vodka distillers fled and brought their craft to Europe and America. Much of the spirit's global success is due to Vladimir Smirnov. After emigrating to France, the exiled Russian vodka maker teamed up with an American entrepreneur and started a market for vodka in the United States. Smirnoff Vodka was distilled in Connecticut, and by the 1950s a successful advertising campaign had made it a household name.

Vodka's success came faster than anyone at the time likely imagined, though it was not an entirely unknown drink. Cocktails like the Black and White Russian and Bloody Mary were around in the 1930s, and the Moscow Mule was a 1940s drink devised almost solely for marketing purposes. It also didn't take long for the three-martini lunch of the 1950s and 60s to be overtaken by Vodka Martinis (gin's botanicals are much more noticeable on the breath, after all). Sweden's introduction of Explorer Vodka in the 1950s to the international market was well-received but quickly overshadowed by the country's other vodka brand Absolut, which grabbed the spotlight with an innovative and well-executed marketing campaign that continues today.

## VODKA TODAY

Ironically, while it didn't take long for vodka distillers to pop up in all corners of the world, politics kept Polish and Russian vodkas off the global market for some time. Stolichnaya (popularly known as Stoli) was the first Russian-distilled vodka to make it to the USA, and that was due to a deal with Pepsi-Cola that introduced the company's fizzy drink to the Soviet Union. After the Cold War, more traditional brands reached off-licence shelves outside the region, but the market was already saturated with competition.

The 1970s and 80s saw the biggest boom in vodka sales, and much of that is attributed to cocktails. As the most neutral-tasting spirit, vodka works with almost anything – from soft fruits and transparent mixers to heavy flavours like coffee, cream, and tomato. After the Cosmopolitan's feature in HBO's *Sex and the City*, martini menus exploded with vodka-based drinks of every imaginable flavour.

Vodka's popularity has not waned. By 2020, the spirit accounted for a third of all alcohol sales in the USA, and global sales topped $40 billion dollars annually. The number of vodka brands is nearly endless. In 2020, over 1,500 US-made craft vodka brands were available, and a 2022 count on just one popular online off-licence topped 600 brands, with an offering of over 3,200 bottles of vodka.

### FLAVOURED VODKA

Flavoured vodkas are a market unto themselves, and a quick glance at off-licence shelves reveals an array of options. Fruit and vanilla vodkas are standard offerings from vodka companies. When the twenty-first century arrived, countless outlandish flavours – including salmon and bacon – appeared as well. It was a crazy market to keep up with and try to develop cocktails for, though it has quelled considerably. Only a handful, such as cake, caramel, chocolate, and whipped cream, remain and even those have been eliminated from many brand portfolios.

There are two distinct ways by which flavour is added to vodka. Technically, 'flavoured vodka' uses the chemistry of natural and artificial ingredients to obtain the desired taste. It was the standard approach for years. These often include some sort of sweetener and are recognizable because they're typically 35 per cent ABV (70 proof). The alternative is 'infused vodka', which introduces natural flavouring ingredients at some point in the distillation process; either via steam in the still (similar to gin) or by steeping the ingredient in the vodka. The latter is how homemade infusions are created. Consumer demand is changing the focus towards natural infusions, so more of these (often labelled 'botanically infused') will appear on the market in years to come.

# TIPS FOR PERFECT COCKTAILS

Crafting a great cocktail is not difficult, it simply requires a few fundamentals, some high-quality ingredients, and the willingness to enjoy the experience – even if every drink doesn't come out exactly as planned. It's just like cooking, putting a bunch of things together to create a balanced, uniformed flavour, only you're dealing with liquids and each drink mixes up in minutes, so honing your skills is much quicker.

Several elements go into cocktails but a few steps will elevate every drink. Fresh ingredients – most importantly citrus juices, which appear frequently – and top-shelf distilled spirits are good places to start. This includes the accent liqueurs like triple sec, because the cheapest options can easily ruin an otherwise splendid drink. However, you don't need to spend a fortune on vodka because there are some fantastic brands that make this spirit worthy of nearly any cocktail. You'll also want to pay attention to ice (see page 12), enhance cocktails with bitters and garnishes, and a small investment in a bit of barware makes each task a little easier. So here's a round up of the key things to consider when you're trying to concoct the perfect cocktail.

## BAR GEAR

A basic bar setup needs only a handful of tools, and the most important of these is a cocktail shaker. The options include a three-piece cobbler shaker with a built-in strainer, or a Boston shaker, which includes a pint-sized glass and mixing tin. For the latter, you'll need a separate strainer; the Hawthorne strainer (the style with a coil underneath) is the most versatile for beginners and the majority of cocktails. Without a shaker, a two-pint Mason jar with a good lid works, though you'll need some sort of strainer to keep ice and solid ingredients out of drinks when desired.

Balanced cocktails are created when the ingredients are properly measured, and the pro bartender's tool for the job is a thimble measure or jigger. This unassuming device has a cup on each end, and the volumes vary slightly. One cup measures a full shot – 45–60ml (1½ or 2fl oz), and the other a half-shot 22 or 30ml (¾ or 1fl oz).

Finally, I highly recommend a long bar spoon, as this will make stirring more efficient, and a muddler to mash fresh ingredients.

## ICE

Unless it's a hot cocktail, ice is essential in almost every drink recipe. It chills the drink, softens the alcohol, and marries all the flavours. The agitation from mixing breaks down the ice, and that dilution is essential for a well-balanced drink that isn't too strong. It's especially important with martini-style cocktails that are made primarily of alcohol, because the point is to enjoy a great drink, not to get drunk.

Keep a regular rotation of ice in the freezer and use only filtered or distilled water to make cubes. Ice does go bad and it will pick up the flavour and aroma of nearby food, especially fish. For best results, use ice within a week or replace it, and have plenty on hand. On average, each drink requires at least five standard ice cubes, though some need more.

## SHAKING AND STIRRING

Shaking and stirring are the two basic mixing techniques, and they're both incredibly easy to master. The general rule is to shake cocktails that include flavourful non-alcoholic mixers like fruit juices and to stir drinks comprised mostly of alcohol or that are mixed in the serving glass.

To shake cocktails, add the ingredients to the shaker then fill it with five or six ice cubes. Shake vigorously for at least 10 seconds, or until the shaker gets frosty. Shake cocktails with heavy ingredients (such as cream, egg, etc.) for up to 30 seconds. Use both hands and hold all the pieces of the shaker firmly so they don't come apart and make a mess.

For stirred cocktails, a bar spoon's long, twisted shaft reaches to the bottom of shakers and tall glasses. Hold the spoon near the top between your thumb and first two fingers and dunk it deep into the ice, then rotate your wrist as you twist the spoon around the glass's circumference for 30 seconds.

With either technique, straining is necessary unless the drink is built directly in the glass. Always strain over fresh ice because the mixing ice will melt faster and water down the drink. Straining also keeps pieces of herbs and fruits out of the drink, and fine-straining is required for the tiniest bits. To do this, use your regular strainer while pouring through a fine-mesh strainer held over the glass.

## MUDDLING

Muddling is an easy, efficient way to extract flavour from fresh ingredients, including fruits and herbs. The tool of choice is a small baton called a muddler or cocktail masher. The flat end goes into the bottom of the glass or shaker and often has a tooth pattern that more effectively smashes ingredients. Plastic cocktail shakers are not great for muddling because they might crack from the force; use stainless-steel or glass vessels.

To muddle, place the muddling ingredients in a shaker or glass and grip the round end of the muddler in your palm. Press it into the ingredients as you twist the muddler five to ten times, depending on the ingredients – softer ingredients require less pressure while harder ingredients will need a little extra work. Add all the other ingredients and the ice, shake or stir, then strain the drink.

## BLENDING

Frozen cocktails are equally simple. Essentially, you'll add ingredients to the blender, turn it on, and blend until everything becomes one slushy or creamy delight. The ice becomes part of the drink, so the quality of your ice is even more important. In some recipes, it's paired with ice cream for more of a milkshake.

For best results, start with crushed ice. Breaking down ice cubes takes a lot more work and can overmix the other ingredients. Place a handful of ice cubes in the blender, chop them into fine pieces, then drain off any excess water before blending the drink. About one cup of crushed ice is perfect for one drink. Switching from fresh to frozen fruits will require a little less ice, so start with about half the amount, then add more and blend again until it reaches your desired consistency.

## GLASSWARE

A variety of glassware provides the opportunity to serve cocktails as intended. For instance, the cocktail (or martini) glass is used for small-volume neat drinks, while a Champagne flute is designed to maximize the bubbles of sparkling wine. Going with classic stemware designs prevents your body heat from warming up the drink prematurely.

Short drinks served on the rocks typically use a small tumbler called an old-fashioned (or rocks) glass. More versatile, because it doesn't need to be filled all the way, is the double old-fashioned glass, which is preferred when a drink is topped with a mixer. Collins and highball glasses are for tall drinks – both are skinny and designed to be filled to the top with ice cubes. Each holds less than 285ml (10fl oz), which is a smaller volume than the average water or fruit juice glass. If you use those as a substitute, understand that the drink likely won't fill the glass

To improve any drink, match the drink and glass temperature. For cold drinks, chill glasses in the freezer for at least 30 minutes or fill them with ice for a few minutes. When making warm cocktails, fill the glass with hot water for a few minutes, dump it, then build the drink.

## PUNCHES

When you need to serve drinks to a crowd at a party, a punch is the easiest option. Punch can be made in advance, and chilling it for an hour or overnight allows the various ingredients to become one cohesive flavour. Just be sure to hold any carbonated elements until it's time to serve so that guests can enjoy the full sparkle.

Serve punch in a pitcher or traditional punchbowl. Adding ice keeps it chilled longer and slightly dilutes the drink. Punch is often best when poured into ice-filled glasses, and this is also an opportunity to impress everyone with lots of garnishes, and the more fruits the better. If you prefer to measure high-volume drinks by the cup, this will help you to convert the recipes in this book:

120ml (4fl oz) = 75g (½ cup)
180ml (6fl oz) = 22g (¾ cup)
240ml (8fl oz) = 150g (1 cup)
360ml (12fl oz) = 225g (1½ cups)
480ml (16fl oz) = 300g (2 cups)

## GARNISHES

When making a drink at home, it's easy to skip the garnish, but adding a few fruits and herbs goes beyond presentation. Squeezing a bit more juice from a lime wedge into the Vodka Tonic or expressing the oils from a lemon twist into martinis adds a subtle kick to drinks. Some garnishes rest in the drink and slowly infuse it with flavour.

Citrus fruits are the most common garnishes, and practicing how to cut slices, wedges, and twists with your own drinks ensures you'll have the skill mastered when it's time to entertain. The flesh of some fruits (such as apple, peach, and pear) turns brown once cut and exposed to oxygen in the air, so to keep them looking great, immediately squirt a little lemon juice onto each slice. Tropical drinks are a fun place to use a pineapple wedge, and skewering a cherry into it creates a 'flag'. Berries and pomegranate arils can be dropped into the drink, while a herb sprig just needs to be poked into the ice.

It's also fun to coat the rim of a glass for extra flavour in each sip. Salt and sugar are most commonly used for margaritas, though there are other options, like the Chocolate Martini's cocoa (page 44) and the Peach Cobbler's brown sugar and graham cracker rim (page 103). With any rimmer, wet the glass rim with a drink ingredient (for instance, run a lime wedge around the glass or dip the rim into a small dish of liqueur or syrup). Keep the glass upside down as you roll or dip it into a dish of salt, sugar, or whatever the recipe calls for, then tap off any excess. If you're not sure whether you'll enjoy it, rim only half the glass and sip from either side.

# SWEETENERS

For a balanced flavour, almost every cocktail recipe includes a sweetener. Rather than regular granulated white sugar, superfine sugar is preferred for cold drinks because it dissolves better. Straight honey poses the same issue, so many recipes dilute it with water to create Honey Syrup (see page 115). Simple Syrup is the other option, because it transforms sugar into a liquid, so you'll find many recipes that use this inexpensive sweetener.

Adding flavour is the fun part of simple syrup! Within the book's recipes, you'll find several flavoured syrups you can make. Use the opposite 150g (1-cup) formula for 1:1 Simple Syrup unless the recipe suggests otherwise. Generally, to add flavour to the syrup, you'll add the flavouring ingredient as the syrup simmers, then let it continue to infuse as the syrup cools. When using whole ingredients, straining is necessary; a fine-mesh strainer works great, or you can run it through a single layer of cheesecloth.

- Simple Syrup: Bring 150g (1 cup) each of water and sugar to a boil, stirring until the sugar dissolves. Simmer for about 5 minutes, then remove from the heat to cool. Bottle it under a tight seal, and store it in the fridge for a week or two.

- Rich Simple Syrup is sweeter and best in drinks that call for plain syrup. This formula is one part water and two parts sugar. For a sugar-free Simple Syrup, use a granulated allulose-based monk fruit sweetener.

## SYRUPS INCLUDED IN THIS BOOK ARE:

**Cinnamon** – Pomegranate Champagne Punch (see page 116)

**Ginger** – Honeydew Frozen Lemonade (see page 47)

**Grapefruit** – Grapefruit Campari Cocktail (see page 40), Pomegranate Fizz (see page 100)

**Lavender** – Vanilla Rose Cocktail (see page 92)

**Rose** – Rosy French 75 (see page 131)

**Rosemary–Basil** – Rosemary and Basil Fizz (see page 79)

**Spiced Syrup**–Peartini (see page 87), Pumpkin Cider (see page 127)

**Honey Syrup**–Sage and Rosemary Bee's Knees (see page 115), Strawberry Vodka Lemonade (see page 124), Kiwi Martini (see page 139)

# INFUSIONS

Vodka infusions are a limitless journey in the cocktail world. It can be a single fruit, herb, or spice, or an infusion that combines complementary flavours. Using fresh ingredients, it's easy to create a flavoured vodka at home that rivals anything you can find at the store. While citrus, berry, pomegranate, and vanilla vodkas are available, there are several infusions that you simply won't find commercially because they're not profitable. Some, such as ginger and pumpkin, do pop up on the market, but if demand is low, even the best-tasting flavoured vodka can disappear.

The process of infusing vodka is pretty simple: add the flavouring ingredients to vodka and let them infuse for several days or weeks. The only work involved is prepping the ingredients, shaking the infusion jar every day or two, and straining once it reaches your ideal flavour intensity.

Many commercial flavoured vodkas are slightly sweetened. You can leave homemade infusions straight or add a bit of syrup. Some flavours, including pumpkin vodka, are best sweet. To do this, start slow and add about 60ml (2fl oz) of Simple Syrup to the strained vodka, shake or stir very well, and add more to taste.

The recipes in this book are designed for a standard bottle of vodka. Any of them are easy to scale back if you don't want to commit to a full bottle or would like to split the vodka and try a few infusions at once. The straight vodkas have an indefinite shelf life when stored at room temperature out of direct sunlight.

Here are a few tips to make the best-quality infusions:

- Use organic produce whenever possible. Alternatively, wash fruits thoroughly to remove any waxy coating or chemicals.

- Most fruit can be sliced or cubed. If the fruit's skin isn't edible, it's best to peel it first and use only the flesh. It's also a good idea to remove all but the tiniest of seeds when possible.

- The time required depends on the ingredient: strong flavours like chili peppers require just an hour, most infusions are ready within a week, and milder flavours such as passion fruit can take up to three weeks.

- During the final few days, check the flavour daily by pouring out a small amount, tasting it, and straining the vodka once you're happy with it.

- It's best to use a cheesecloth-lined fine-mesh strainer to catch the smallest pieces and ensure a clean vodka. Some may need to be strained two or three times.

- Pour the flavoured vodka into a clean bottle with a tight seal (recycled vodka bottles are excellent), label it, and add it to your drinks cabinet. These should be drunk within a year.

## INFUSIONS INCLUDED IN THIS BOOK ARE:

**Apple-Pear-Cinnamon** – Autumn Spiced Tonic (see page 119)

**Blueberry** – Blueberry Bellini (see page 84)

**Chilli-citrus** – Spicy Spritzer (see page 60)

**Cinnamon** – Caramel Apple Sangria (see page 64)

**Citrus** – Cosmopolitan (see page 27), White Cosmo (see page 75), Pomegranate Champagne Punch (see page 116)

**Coconut** – Lychee Ginger Martini (see page 71), Coconut Sex on the Beach (see page 48), Coconut and Mango Frosé (see page 68), Lava Flow Cocktail (see page 108)

**Cucumber** – Rosemary and Basil Fizz (see page 79)

**Ginger** – Ginger Madras (see page 55), Pomegranate Fizz (see page 100)

**Lemon** – Jasmine Tea Tini (see page 72)

**Passion Fruit** – Passion Pearl Cocktail (see page 91)

**Peach** – Peach Cobbler (see page 103)

**Pear** – Christmas Mule (see page 120), Daphne Martini (see page 104), Peartini (see page 87)

**Pineapple** – Pineapple Mimosa (see page 132)

**Pomegranate** – Cider Delight (see page 99)

**Raspberry** – Sparkling Raspberry Press (see page 63), Gummy Bear Martini (see page 112), Sparkling Melon Punch (see page 67)

**Rosemary** – Vanilla Rose Cocktail (see page 92)

**Vanilla** – Chocolate Martini (see page 44), Sugar Cookie Martini (see page 39), Light Coconut Martini (see page 83), Strawberry Vodka Lemonade (see page 124), Spiked Arnold Palmer (see page 123), Spiked Caramel Latte (see page 107), Sparkling Melon Punch (see page 67), Rosy French 75 (see page 131)

# THE RECIPES

# VODKA MARTINI

The Vodka Martini is a fantastic cocktail that is incredibly simple yet wonderfully satisfying. It's the ideal place to showcase the best vodka you can afford, and it's a drink that you can adapt to perfectly suit your own taste. Nothing more than vodka, dry vermouth, and bitters, the Vodka Martini is most often shaken, though you can stir it if you please. Using less vermouth creates more of a vodka-forward, transparently flavoured cocktail, while the full pour of vermouth adds a nice herbal note. For a subtle accent, switch from aromatic to orange bitters, or have fun exploring other flavours of this essential cocktail enhancer, including celery, lavender, and rhubarb bitters. The garnish also transforms the drink into a new delight: a simple lemon twist offers a bright citrus touch, while a few olives infuse it with a briny, more savoury flavour.

### Ingredients
60ml (2fl oz) vodka
15–22ml (½–¾fl oz) dry vermouth
2 dashes of aromatic bitters
a lemon twist or 3 olives on a skewer, to garnish

### Instructions
Pour the vodka, dry vermouth, and bitters into a cocktail shaker and fill it with ice. Shake well and strain into a chilled cocktail glass, garnishing the drink with a lemon twist or a skewer of olives.

*Tip:* Be sure that your vermouth is fresh – once open, keep the bottle refrigerated and finish it within three months.

# LEMON DROP MARTINI

When you're in the mood for a tart, lemonade-like martini, the Lemon Drop is sure to please. Quick to mix, there's something special about this three-ingredient cocktail, which is why it's a staple on the modern martini menu. The keys to this recipe are freshly squeezed lemon juice and homemade Rich Simple Syrup (see page 17). It's also highly adaptable to your own taste. If you enjoy a tart drink, use just a bit of Rich Simple Syrup, or pour a little extra when you want a more equal balance of sweet and tart. Rimming the glass with sugar adds to the drink's candy-like taste and makes each sip a little sweeter.

### Ingredients
lemon wedge and superfine sugar, for decorating the glass
60ml (2fl oz) vodka
30ml (1fl oz) fresh lemon juice
15–22ml (½–¾fl oz) Rich Simple Syrup (see page 17), to taste
a lemon twist, to garnish

### Instructions
Coat the rim of a cocktail glass by running a lemon wedge around it, then dipping the wet glass into a shallow dish of superfine sugar. Into a cocktail shaker, pour the vodka, lemon juice, and Rich Simple Syrup, then fill it with ice and shake well. Strain into the prepared glass and garnish with a lemon twist.

# COSMOPOLITAN

Popularly called the 'Cosmo', this is arguably the most famous vodka martini. It's often the 'gateway' drink that leads imbibers to other fancy cocktails, including the drier classics. Much of that has to do with its role in the *Sex and the City* series, though there's so much to love about this cranberry-kissed twist on the Kamikaze cocktail. It's an iconic American cocktail that was likely created in the mid-1970s from a basic formula of Citrus Vodka, Cointreau (or another top-shelf triple sec), and lime and cranberry juices. This recipe is a classically styled, drier Cosmo that uses less cranberry than some modern renditions, which should mix up to a pretty, pale-pink colour. To make it sweeter and a deeper shade of red, pour in up to 22ml (¾fl oz) of cranberry juice.

### Ingredients
45ml (1½fl oz) Citrus Vodka (see below)
30ml (1fl oz) Cointreau
15ml (½fl oz) fresh lime juice
8ml (¼fl oz) cranberry juice
a slither of orange peel, to garnish

### Instructions
Into a cocktail shaker, pour the Citrus Vodka, Cointreau, lime juice, and cranberry juice. Fill the shaker with ice and shake well. Strain into a chilled cocktail glass and garnish with the slither of orange peel.

***Citrus Vodka:*** Infuse a blend of citrus peels – 14g (½oz) each of organic lemon and orange peels is a good mix – in a clean infusion jar with a lid, cover with 735ml (25fl oz) of vodka seal, and leave to infuse for 5 to 7 days before using.

# WHITE RUSSIAN

Before vodka was a household name in the United States, several brands and bartenders worked together to devise ingenious marketing plans that would sell the novel spirits to Americans. They often took on Russian-inspired names because the country was among the first to export the clear spirit to the USA in the early to mid-twentieth century. The White Russian became one of the most enduring of these concoctions, and it remains a favourite decades later. A simple mix that's served on the rocks, this easy-sipping drink flavours vodka with coffee liqueur and a bit of cream. While you can shake it for more of a coffee-flavoured, milkshake-like taste, it's fabulous when built right in the glass. Float the cream on top by pouring it over the back of a spoon for a fantastic presentation, then let each drinker stir it in as desired. Plant-based milk works great as a cream substitute (particularly vanilla-flavoured soy or almond milk), or you can skip the cream entirely to make a Black Russian.

### Ingredients
45ml (1½fl oz) vodka
22ml (¾fl oz) coffee liqueur
22ml (¾fl oz) cream

### Instructions
Into an old-fashioned glass filled with ice, pour the vodka and coffee liqueur. Stir well. Slowly pour the cream over the back of a spoon so it floats on top. Serve with a straw and stir as you drink.

# APPLE MARTINI

Apple Martinis (or Appletinis, if you prefer) can be made with apple juice or cider, but there's a certain allure to the recipes that feature sour apple schnapps. The liqueur is both sweet and sour, and it creates an eye-catching green cocktail that is sure to tantalize your tastebuds. With the high-alcohol kick of vodka in the background, this recipe gets a little extra tartness from fresh lemon juice, though it shouldn't be enough to make you pucker. If you want a slightly softer drink, add the optional Simple Syrup to the shaker. For a stunning garnish, skewer a few thin green apple slices and layer them into a fan. Don't forget to use lemon juice to keep the slices looking fresh (see page 16).

### Ingredients
45ml (1½fl oz) vodka
15ml (½fl oz) sour apple schnapps
8ml (¼fl oz) fresh lemon juice
a dash of Rich Simple Syrup (see page 17), (optional)
thin green apple slices, to garnish

### Instructions
Into a cocktail shaker, pour the vodka, apple schnapps, lemon juice, and Rich Simple Syrup, if using. Fill the shaker with ice and shake well. Strain into a chilled cocktail glass and garnish with the apple slices.

# CAPE COD

In a younger crowd, you'll likely hear this drink called a
vodka cranberry or vodka cran, but to old-school bartenders
and vodka drinkers, it's the Cape Cod (sometimes Codder).
By any name, it's difficult to resist a juicy highball that
requires just two ingredients. Any vodka will do just fine here,
and since cranberry juice is so flavourful, there's no need
to pour your best spirit. It's also a great opportunity to play
with other fruit juices. For instance, split the cranberry with
pineapple juice for a Bay Breeze, grapefruit juice for a Sea
Breeze, or orange juice for a Madras. With any of these,
adding a squeeze of lime juice every now and then brightens
up the drink wonderfully, so consider the garnish necessary.

### Ingredients
60ml (2fl oz) vodka
90–150ml (3–5fl oz) cranberry juice, to taste
a lime wedge, to garnish

### Instructions
Into a highball glass filled with ice, pour the vodka
and cranberry juice. Garnish with a lime wedge.

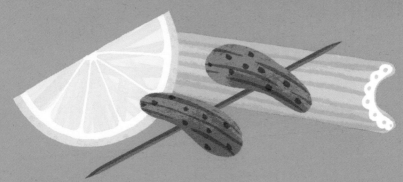

# BLOODY MARY

The Bloody Mary is a favourite cold-weather drink, and it makes a fabulous mid-morning cocktail, too. Likely created in the 1920s at the ex-pat Paris establishment, Harry's New York Bar, the true beauty of this savoury beverage is its adaptability. Include all of the flavouring ingredients, make it as spicy as you like and feel free to do it up with crazy garnishes – everything from shrimp to mini grilled-cheese sandwiches on skewers can be found in this one.

### Ingredients
45ml (1½fl oz) vodka
90ml (3fl oz) tomato juice
15ml (½fl oz) fresh lemon juice
a dash of Worcestershire sauce
a dash of hot sauce
a pinch of celery salt
a pinch of black pepper
¼ teaspoon horseradish (optional)
a lemon wedge, celery stalk, sliced gherkin, to garnish

### Instructions
Into a highball glass filled with ice, pour the vodka, tomato juice and lemon juice. Add the remaining ingredients and stir for at least 30 seconds. Garnish with a lemon wedge, celery stalk, and sliced gherkin.

*Tip:* To make an 8-serving pitcher, make the Bloody Mary mix by combining 600g (4 cups) of tomato juice, 75g (½ cup) of lemon juice, ½ teaspoon each of Worcestershire sauce, hot sauce, celery salt, and freshly ground black pepper. Stir the mix well and refrigerate for up to one week. When ready to serve, add 45ml (1½fl oz) of vodka to each ice-filled tall glass, pouring 150–180ml (5–6fl oz) of Bloody Mary mix.

# MOSCOW MULE

Drinks like the Moscow Mule propelled vodka to stardom in the bar. While this cocktail has seen a modern brush with fame, it's been around since the 1940s and was literally created to sell vodka to American drinkers. Thanks to a brilliant marketing campaign, decades later we have this snappy vodka and ginger beer drink to enjoy. It's refreshingly simple and a great use for your favourite budget-friendly vodka. The mule is also an opportunity to explore the array of ginger beers available; some are sweet, some very spicy, and some fall in between. You can also go down the traditional route and serve this in a copper mug, though it's just as pleasant in a large glass tumbler.

### Ingredients
60ml (2fl oz) vodka
15ml (½fl oz) fresh lime juice
120ml (4fl oz) ginger beer
a lime wedge, to garnish

### Instructions
Fill a copper mug or double old-fashioned glass with ice, then pour over the vodka and lime juice. Top up with the ginger beer and garnish with a lime wedge.

# SUGAR COOKIE MARTINI

Sometimes you simply want to indulge in a sweet treat. Rather than whipping up a batch of baked goodies, shake up this simple Sugar Cookie Martini. It's not quite as sweet as its namesake and doesn't accurately replicate a cookie, but it is an utterly delicious, creamy cocktail, and the frosting rim with colourful sugar strands is a lot of fun. Three common bar ingredients go into the shaker – Vanilla Vodka (see below for a homemade infusion), Irish cream, and amaretto – and that makes it even easier. If you want to skip the frosting, dip the glass rim into a small dish of either liqueur.

### Ingredients
45ml (1½fl oz) Vanilla Vodka (see below)
45ml (1½fl oz) Irish cream liqueur
30ml (1fl oz)  amaretto liqueur
vanilla frosting and coloured sugar strands,
to decorate the glass

### Instructions
Dip the rim of the cocktail glass into a dish of vanilla frosting, rolling it around to get a good coating. Then dip the frosted glass into a second small dish filled with coloured sugar strands to stick them to the edge. Pour the spirits into a cocktail shaker, fill with ice and shake, then strain into the prepared glass.

***Vanilla Vodka:*** To make Vanilla Vodka, split a vanilla bean lengthwise and infuse it in a clean infusion jar with a lid, cover with 735ml (25fl oz) of vodka, seal and leave to infuse for 3–4 days before using.

**39**

# GRAPEFRUIT CAMPARI COCKTAIL

Vodka's neutral taste makes it the perfect vehicle for an array of flavours, and that includes the bitter taste of Campari. The two are often paired in apéritif cocktails; one of the better known of which is simply called the Campari Cocktail. Grapefruit is a natural complement to the bitter's unique, orange-dominant flavour. Mixing that juice into a syrup offsets the spirit's bitterness with a sweet citrus touch that results in an intriguing dinner refreshment the average drinker may find more approachable. While it is typically served up like a martini, you can transform it into a refreshing tall drink by straining the shaken mix over ice and topping it up with seltzer or soda water.

### Ingredients
22ml (¾fl oz) vodka
30ml (1fl oz) Campari
15ml (½fl oz) Grapefruit Simple Syrup (see below)
1–2 dashes of aromatic bitters
a grapefruit twist, to garnish

### Instructions
Into a mixing glass filled with ice, pour the vodka, Campari, Grapefruit Simple Syrup, and bitters and stir to mix for about 30 seconds. Strain into a cocktail glass and garnish with a grapefruit twist.

***Grapefruit Simple Syrup:*** Add 90ml (3fl oz) of fresh grapefruit juice to the standard Simple Syrup recipe (see page 17) after you have removed it from the heat.

# SCREWDRIVER

A truly basic cocktail, anyone can make a Screwdriver. Simply top a shot of vodka with orange juice and enjoy! While that's easy enough, there are also delicious ways to make it an even better drink. Think about using a flavoured vodka – raspberry, pomegranate, and vanilla are great commercial options – or play around with homemade herb-infused vodka (basil and rosemary are particularly well-suited to orange juice). No matter which vodka you pour, the real key to a superb Screwdriver is freshly squeezed OJ, and you'll need about 2 medium-sized oranges for one drink. A few minutes of effort will be repaid with each sip. If orange juice is a bit too acidic for your taste, a splash of Simple Syrup (see page 17) or grenadine (for a tequila sunrise effect) will sweeten it right up.

### Ingredients
60ml (2fl oz) vodka
150ml (5fl oz) fresh orange juice
an orange slice, to garnish

### Instructions
Into a tall glass filled with ice, pour the vodka and orange juice. Stir well and garnish with an orange slice.

# CHOCOLATE MARTINI

Sweet and utterly delicious, there are several ways to make a Chocolate Martini. As much as this staple of the modern cocktail menu has been reinvented over the last few decades, there's something satisfying about this drink, as one of the first versions of the original martini. Rather than being loaded up with cream and other indulgent ingredients, this Chocolate Martini opts for a far more subtle approach, using crème de cacao, a super sweet cocoa-infused liqueur. It works with either white (clear) or dark crème de cacao, and which one you pour will affect the drink's colour but not the taste. For a boost of flavour and an extra dimension, the liqueur is paired with Vanilla Vodka and chocolate bitters, and dusting the glass rim with cocoa powder sweetens each sip wonderfully.

### Ingredients
45ml (1 ½fl oz) crème de cacao
60ml (2fl oz) Vanilla Vodka (see 39)
2 dashes of chocolate bitters
cocoa powder, for decorating the glass

### Instructions
Prepare two shallow dishes; one with a small amount of crème de cacao, the other with cocoa powder. Wet the rim of a cocktail glass in the chocolate liqueur, then immediately dip the wet glass into a small dish of cocoa powder. Add the Vanilla Vodka and crème de cacao to a cocktail shaker and fill it with ice. Shake well and strain into the prepared glass, then add the chocolate bitters.

# HONEYDEW FROZEN LEMONADE

Frozen lemonade is a dreamy way to cool down on a hot day. In the Honeydew Frozen Lemonade, the sweet melon and spiced tartness of Ginger Lemonade are married with raspberry liqueur – floating the liqueur on top adds a dark layer that stands out against the pale drink. The Ginger Lemonade is easy to make by the pitcher and delicious on its own.

### Ingredients
75g (½ cup) honeydew melon cubes or balls
45ml (1½fl oz) vodka
90ml (3fl oz) Ginger Lemonade (see below)
150g (1 cup) crushed ice
15ml (½fl oz) raspberry liqueur
honeydew melon balls on a skewer, to garnish

### Instructions
Add the melon, vodka, Ginger Lemonade, and ice to a blender and blend until smooth. Pour into a tall glass, and float raspberry liqueur on top by pouring it slowly over the back of a bar spoon or teaspoon, garnishing with a skewer of honeydew melon balls.

*Ginger Lemonade:* To make 4 pints (2 quarts): mix a Ginger Syrup by putting 480ml (16fl oz) water, 150g (1 cup) raw sugar, and 150g (1 cup) peeled and chopped fresh ginger into a saucepan. Cover, simmer over a medium heat for 15 minutes, then cool completely before straining. Combine 360ml (12fl oz) Ginger Syrup with 360ml (12fl oz) fresh lemon juice, and 945ml (32fl oz) water. Stir, add more of any ingredient to taste, then chill for at least 1 hour. It keeps well for up to a week.

**47**

# COCONUT SEX ON THE BEACH

Straight out of the 1980s, when you're looking for the ultimate throwback cocktail, mix up a Sex on the Beach. It's a favourite bar drink that has been remade countless times, and this version adds a Coconut Vodka (see page 71 for a homemade infusion) twist to the orange-cranberry juice drink. Beyond the vodka, the drink is spiked with peach schnapps and crème de cassis (a sweet, blackcurrant-flavoured liqueur), and it all comes together to create a delightfully fruity drink. In lieu of Coconut Vodka, add 15ml (½fl oz) of coconut water and reduce the orange juice to 45ml (1½fl oz). You can also lighten up the drink by switching to white cranberry juice or topping it with sparkling water, or a light fizzy drink will work as long as it isn't too sweet, because the liqueurs take care of that aspect.

## Ingredients
45ml (1½fl oz) Coconut Vodka (see page 71)
22ml (¾fl oz) peach schnapps
15ml (½fl oz) crème de cassis
60ml (2fl oz) fresh orange juice
60ml (2fl oz) cranberry juice
a maraschino cherry and ½ orange slice, to garnish

## Instructions
Fill a tall glass with ice and pour in all of the ingredients. Stir very well to combine, then add the fruit and serve.

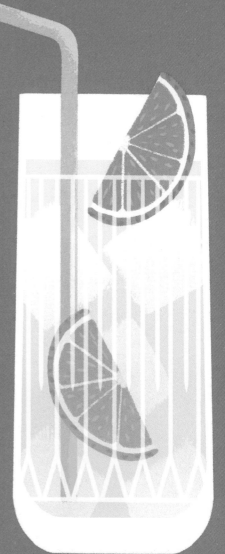

# VODKA TONIC

Modern fizzy drinks are often very sweet. When you want to cut the sugar but still enjoy a sparkling mixed drink, tonic water is the way to go. Cinchona bark is responsible for its semi-dry bitter taste, and several manufacturers make fantastic tonic waters. Add a shot of vodka and a squeeze of fresh lime and you have a vodka tonic! It's a fantastic dinner drink that goes with everything from hearty Italian pasta dishes to spicy Asian foods, and a wonderful refreshment for any afternoon. With any tonic drink, I like to serve a few lime wedges; drop one or two into the glass and save one for a garnish. When you want to add a tart kick to the drink, wipe the lime wedge for the garnish around the glass rim then squeeze the excess juice into the drink.

### Ingredients
60ml (2fl oz) vodka
8ml (¼fl oz) fresh lime juice
120–180ml (4–6fl oz) tonic water
2–3 lime wedges, to garnish

### Instructions
Into a highball glass filled with ice, pour the vodka and lime juice. Top up with tonic water to your preferred dilution and garnish with a few lime wedges.

# MANGO VODKA COLLINS

The Collins family of mixed drinks famously includes whisky (John Collins) and gin (Tom Collins) versions, and the Vodka Collins is a close third. The formula for all of these is a shot of the base spirit accented with lemon juice and Simple Syrup, then topped with soda. They're all refreshing and a wonderful base for other drinks, with a few adjustments and additions. In this mango version, a bit of mango nectar adds a tropical fruit twist and bright yellow colour. It's a fantastic option for hot days. The nectar is relatively easy to find at supermarkets and natural food shops.

### Ingredients
45ml (1 ½fl oz) vodka
15ml (½fl oz) fresh lemon juice
15ml (½fl oz) mango nectar
15ml (½fl oz) Rich Simple Syrup (see page 17)
90–150ml (3–5fl oz) soda water, to taste
a mango or lemon slice, to garnish

### Instructions
Into a highball glass filled with ice, pour the vodka, lemon juice, mango nectar, and Simple Syrup. Stir well, then top up with soda water. Garnish with a mango or lemon slice.

# GINGER MADRAS

Building on the popular combination of vodka and cranberry (see Cape Cod, page 32), there is a series of juicy trios that bring extra fruit into the mix. The Madras is cranberry and orange, the Bay Breeze uses cranberry and pineapple, and the Sea Breeze pairs cranberry with grapefruit. All of these fruity highballs make perfect additions to a Ginger Vodka base. The extra flavour from this simple infusion (it's not the easiest to find commercially, so it's likely a DIY project) adds dimension, and each fruit pairs wonderfully with ginger's snappy spice. Enjoy this spiced version of the Madras, then try the other two by substituting the secondary fruit juice with each drink's distinguishing ingredient, and switch up the citrus garnish to match. Adding a few cranberries for the garnish gives this a seasonal touch when serving it at winter events.

### Ingredients
45ml (1½fl oz) Ginger Vodka (see below)
90ml (3fl oz) cranberry juice
90ml (3fl oz) fresh orange juice
an orange slice or a few cranberries, to garnish

### Instructions
Fill a highball glass with ice, then pour in the Ginger Vodka and fruit juices. Stir well and garnish with the fruit.

*Ginger Vodka:* Add about 75g (½ cup) of sliced ginger (peel non-organic ginger first) to a clean infusion jar with a lid, cover with 735ml (25fl oz) of vodka, seal, and leave to infuse for 1–2 weeks.

**55**

# PAPAYA KAMIKAZE

The Kamikaze was created in the mid-twentieth century and it's vodka's answer to the original lime-flavoured margarita and daiquiri. This iconic bar drink is also incredibly easy to make because it requires just three common ingredients. Building on the base of vodka, triple sec, and lime juice, you can give it a renewed flair by introducing an additional fruit. In this case, you'll muddle (see page 13) fresh papaya into the mix to create a tasty Papaya Kamikaze. The fruit is a brilliant complement to lime and is a welcome addition to this popular cocktail.

### Ingredients
2 slices of fresh papaya
30ml (1fl oz) fresh lime juice
45ml (1½fl oz) vodka
30ml (1fl oz) triple sec
a lime slice, to garnish

### Instructions
In the bottom of a cocktail shaker, muddle the fresh papaya and lime juice. Add the vodka and triple sec, then fill the shaker with ice and shake well. Fine-strain into a chilled cocktail glass and garnish with the lime slice.

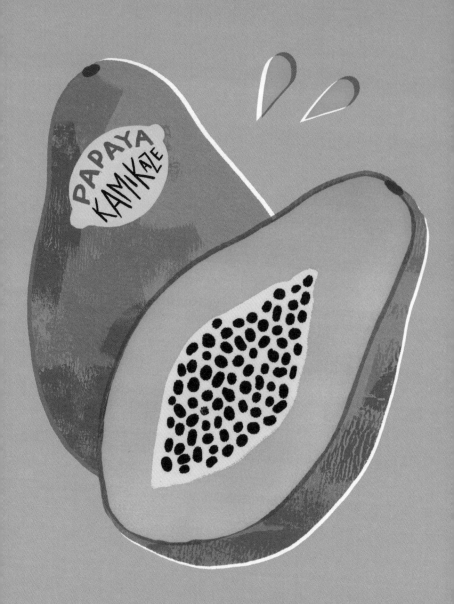

**COFFEE**

*WAKE ME UP BREW*

TRIPLE
DISTILLED
VODKA

40% ALC
1 Lt

# ESPRESSO MARTINI

For a spiked afternoon pick-me-up, few drinks can beat
the Espresso Martini. There are several approaches to this
drink, though as any coffee lover knows, it's hard to match
the taste of freshly brewed espresso (if you don't have an
espresso machine, a moka pot is a good alternative). This
martini mixes vodka and coffee liqueur with chilled espresso
and adds a touch of chocolate for a mocha-like taste.
When shaken, you'll often get a foamy top reminiscent of
the crema on top of freshly pulled espresso shots. Stick with
regular vodka or build on the coffee flavour with espresso
vodka. Vanilla Vodka (see page 39) is a fun option as well.

### Ingredients
45ml (1 ½fl oz) vodka
22ml (¾fl oz) coffee liqueur
8ml (¼fl oz) crème de cacao
30ml (1 fl oz) chilled espresso
3 coffee beans, to garnish

### Instructions
Pour the vodka, liqueurs and espresso into a cocktail
shaker, then fill it with ice. Shake vigorously and strain into
a chilled cocktail glass. Garnish with a few coffee beans.

# SPICY SPRITZER

Wine spritzers are extremely simple drinks. Traditionally made with nothing more than white wine and soda water, they're also very refreshing. There are many ways that you can adapt that basic formula to create exciting new drinks, and this Spicy Spritzer is definitely a fun option, especially if you want to add a little spice to your cocktail routine. It requires a quick chilli-pepper infusion in citrus-flavoured vodka, and Thai chillies and jalapeños work best. Simply place a couple of peppers in the amount of vodka you want to infuse for an hour or two, and taste it regularly so it doesn't get too hot. Once it's ready, mix the spicy vodka with white wine (rosé wines work great, too) and soda water. To maintain a balance of flavour, use soda water with sweeter wine and ginger ale with a drier wine.

### Ingredients
45ml (1 ½fl oz) Chilli-infused Citrus Vodka (see below)
90ml (3fl oz) white wine
a splash of soda water or ginger ale
an orange slice, to garnish

### Instructions
Pour the infused vodka and wine into an old-fashioned glass filled with ice. Top with soda water or ginger ale, stir, and garnish with an orange slice.

*Chilli-infused Citrus Vodka:* Add one or two hot chilli peppers to a clean infusion jar with a lid, cover with 735ml (25fl oz) of Citrus Vodka, seal, and leave to infuse for 1–2 hours (test it frequently). If you want to make your own Citrus Vodka (see page 27), perfect that infusion first, then add the chilli peppers.

# SPARKLING RASPBERRY PRESS

The Vodka Press is a refreshing highball that mixes two sodas. It's a variation on the Presbyterian, which uses whisky with soda water and lemon-lime soda. The Sparkling Raspberry Press adds a spin to the vodka-mixed drink, and it all begins with a muddle of fresh raspberries and lime. To ramp up the flavour it uses a shot of raspberry vodka, and rather than a second soda, sparkling rosé or white wine gives it new vibrancy. 'Press' drinks are most commonly made with a bartending technique called 'rolling', which is done by pouring the drink between two glasses. Pint and mixing glasses are the best choices; just be sure to use glasses that hold the same volume and to leave a little headroom at the top to avoid spills. It requires a bit of attention and practise, though you can stir the drink if you prefer.

### Ingredients
5–6 raspberries
2 lime slices
60ml (2fl oz) Raspberry Vodka (see page 112)
60ml (2fl oz) sparkling wine
60ml (2fl oz) soda water
fresh raspberries and lime slices, to garnish

### Instructions
In the bottom of a highball glass, muddle the raspberries and lime slices. Fill the glass partially with ice, add the vodka, wine, and soda water, then roll the drink (or stir). If needed, add a couple more ice cubes before serving, then garnish with more raspberries and slices of lime.

# CARAMEL APPLE SANGRIA
(Serves 10)

Sangria is a fabulous party drink that's easily adaptable to any occasion. When you're entertaining in the autumn, mix up a pitcher of Caramel Apple Sangria for your guests. Sure to please anyone, it sweetens apple cider with caramel syrup to capture the best taste of the season, then adds interest with a combination of vodka and sparkling wine. Apple cider is at its prime when fresh-pressed. It's typically cloudier than the average bottled apple cider and should be kept cold or refrigerated, unless the maker includes preservatives. Look for the syrup among coffee sweeteners at your local shop.

### Ingredients
240ml (8fl oz) Cinnamon Vodka (see below)
60ml (2fl oz) caramel syrup
720ml (24fl oz) non-alcoholic apple cider
3 red apples, cored and sliced
1 bottle of sparkling wine
a few apple slices, to garnish

### Instructions
In a pitcher, combine the vodka, syrup, and cider. Stir well, ensuring the syrup is thoroughly mixed into the liquid. Add the apple slices and refrigerate overnight. Just before serving, add the sparkling wine. Serve in stemmed wine glasses (over ice if you prefer) and garnish with apple slices.

***Cinnamon Vodka:*** Add 2 cinnamon sticks to a clean infusion jar with a lid, cover with 735ml (25fl oz) of vodka, seal, and leave to infuse for 3–4 days.

**64**

# SPARKLING MELON PUNCH
(Serves 8–10)

Bright green, the Sparkling Melon Punch is sure to grab anyone's attention. It's an easy last-minute party punch that looks great in a pitcher or punchbowl, and the red strawberries are a fun addition for their flavour and contrasting colour. The punch is focused on a green melon liqueur such as Midori, while the background is a combination of Vanilla and Raspberry Vodkas (both of which you can make at home; see pages 39 and 112). To offset all that sweetness, pineapple juice brings in some much-needed tartness. The punch can be quite potent, so a lot of seltzer is required. Not only does this make it more refreshing, but it also knocks down the alcohol content so it's appropriate for a party (about 9% ABV).

## Ingredients
4–5 large strawberries, sliced
90ml (3fl oz) Vanilla Vodka (see page 39)
90ml (3fl oz) Raspberry Vodka (see page 112)
240ml (8fl oz) melon liqueur
180ml (6fl oz) pineapple juice
945ml (32fl oz) seltzer

## Instructions
In a pitcher or punchbowl, combine the strawberries, vodkas, melon liqueur, and pineapple juice. Stir well and add the seltzer just before serving in glasses over ice.

# COCONUT AND MANGO FROSÉ

The Frosé started out as a trendy drink that transformed rosé wine into a delightful frozen cocktail. The wine slushy comes in many flavours – from strawberries to tasty fruity combinations – and has endless possibilities. This Coconut and Mango Frosé is a tropical delight that combines Coconut Vodka with fresh mango or mango nectar. A handful of companies make this flavour of vodka, but it's also a simple homemade infusion (see page 71). For the rosé, look for a wine made with red grapes (e.g., Pinot Noir, Merlot, Tempranillo) as these have a bolder flavour that won't get lost in the blender.

### Ingredients
1 cup of ice
2 slices of fresh mango or 30ml (1fl oz) mango nectar
30ml (1fl oz) Coconut Vodka (see page 71)
90ml (3fl oz) rosé wine
15ml (½fl oz) lemon juice
15ml (½fl oz) Rich Simple Syrup (see page 17)
mango and lemon slices, to garnish

### Instructions
Place the ice and mango flesh or nectar in a blender and chop lightly. Add the other ingredients and blend until smooth. Pour into a stemmed glass and garnish with slices of mango and lemon.
To thicken the Frosé, add more ice (depending on your preference, up to 300g/2 cups) and blend again. If you'd like it a bit sweeter, add an extra splash of syrup. Keep any excess Frosé in the freezer until you're ready for another drink.

LYCHEE

*liqueur*

20% VOL

# LYCHEE GINGER MARTINI

Lychee is a fascinating flavour for cocktails, and it pairs extremely well with coconut and ginger. Also called alligator strawberries because of the fruit's scaly outer skin and strawberry-like taste, lychees are small Asian fruits. You can buy or make either the syrup or liqueur for this sparkling martini recipe. It's mixed with coconut vodka, which a few companies produce, or you can make a quick homemade infusion. Adding ginger ale livens up the mix with a bit more sweetness to finish off this tasty little drink.

## Ingredients
45ml (1½fl oz) lychee liqueur or syrup
45ml (1½fl oz) Coconut Vodka (see below)
45ml (1½fl oz) ginger ale
a lychee or lemon twist, to garnish

## Instructions
Pour the lychee liqueur or syrup and Coconut Vodka into a cocktail shaker filled with ice and shake well. Strain into a chilled cocktail glass, then top up with ginger ale and garnish with a lychee or lemon twist.

***Coconut Vodka:*** Add 75g (½ cup) of unsweetened coconut flakes to a clean infusion jar with a lid, cover with 735ml (25fl oz) of vodka, seal, and leave to infuse for 4–5 days.

# JASMINE TEA TINI

Tea is a fabulous drink mixer, and it's particularly well suited to vodka martinis. The captivating aroma of jasmine tea – most often green tea scented with jasmine blossoms – plays well off a hint of citrus and sweet wine in the Jasmine Tea Tini. Use fresh-brewed tea that's well chilled and add an extra splash of syrup if you have a dry rosé (white wine is great, too). While this version uses Lemon Vodka (a simple one-week infusion), you could also use unflavoured vodka with a splash of lemon juice. It's a lovely pitcher drink when you need to serve a small party, and it should make afternoon tea a bit more interesting, too!

### Ingredients
30ml (1fl oz) Lemon Vodka (see below)
30ml (1fl oz) rosé wine
60ml (2fl oz) jasmine tea, chilled
a splash of Rich Simple Syrup (see page 17)
a jasmine flower or long lemon twist, to garnish

### Instructions
In a cocktail shaker filled with ice, combine all the ingredients. Shake well and strain into a chilled cocktail glass. If available, garnish with a jasmine flower, otherwise use a long lemon twist.

*Make it a pitcher:* Increase each ingredient in proportion to the number of servings needed. Combine them in a pitcher and stir well with ice, then serve in cocktail glasses and garnish.

*Lemon Vodka:* Add 30ml (1fl oz) of organic lemon peels to a clean infusion jar with a lid, cover with 735ml (25fl oz) of vodka, seal, and leave to infuse for 5–7 days.

# WHITE COSMO

The Cosmopolitan has inspired countless cocktail recipes, and the White Cosmo is a delicately sweet version of the fruity martini. It begins with a Citrus Vodka (see page 27 for the homemade infusion) and prefers the lighter flavour of white cranberry juice, which pairs better with lemon rather than the lime of the original cocktail. An elderflower liqueur gives it a floral kiss that's sure to please; St-Germain is the most popular brand, though it is made by other companies, and elderflower cordial is a great substitute. While it's fabulous year-round, sugar-dusted cranberries transform this Cosmo into a delightful holiday cocktail. Feel free to nibble on the garnish because the sweet-tart taste is a fun contrast to the drink.

### Ingredients
45ml (1½fl oz) Citrus Vodka (see page 27)
15ml (½fl oz) elderflower liqueur
30ml (1fl oz) white cranberry juice
8ml (¼fl oz) freshly squeezed lemon juice
3 fresh cranberries and white granulated sugar, to garnish

### Instructions
First prepare the garnish; skewer the cranberries and dust them with sugar, tapping off any excess, then set aside. Pour all the other ingredients into a cocktail shaker, fill with ice, and shake well. Strain into a chilled cocktail glass and garnish with the sugared cranberries.

# KOMBUCHA GREYHOUND

Kombucha is more than a trendy beverage to drink on its own. Whether you brew it at home or pick it up at the shop, the fermented tea drink is an intriguing ingredient. Kombucha is relatively new to the cocktail world, so recipes are scarce, but the best place to start experimentation is with the simplest mixed drinks. In the Kombucha Greyhound, the original drink's perfect combination of vodka and grapefruit juice is enriched with ginger kombucha. The two flavours are ideal companions and kombucha gives the normally juice-forward Greyhound a bright and gentle fizz that's pleasantly refreshing. Go with your preference of white, pink, or ruby red grapefruit; it's best with freshly squeezed juice, and you can get enough for about two drinks from the average grapefruit.

### Ingredients
60ml (2fl oz) vodka
60ml (2fl oz) freshly squeezed grapefruit juice
60ml (2fl oz) ginger kombucha
a small grapefruit wedge, to garnish

### Instructions
Pour the three ingredients into a tall glass filled with ice, stir well, and garnish with the grapefruit wedge.

KOMBU CHA!

ORGANIC

GINGER

GREY HOUND

—VODKA—

# ROSEMARY AND BASIL FIZZ

With a love of gardening comes an appreciation for all things that are made from that homegrown produce. If you're the type of person who's always looking for new ways to enjoy the fruits of your labour, the Rosemary and Basil Fizz is the drink for you. The garden-fresh drink begins with cucumber-infused vodka and the Rosemary-basil Simple Syrup celebrates the taste of fresh herbs. Though it may require a bit of work, this drink is the ultimate refreshment for a warm day in your garden.

### Ingredients
45ml (1½fl oz) Cucumber Vodka (see below)
15ml (½fl oz) lime juice
15ml (½fl oz) Rosemary-basil Simple Syrup (see below)
90ml (3fl oz) soda water or sparkling wine
a fresh rosemary sprig and a lime wedge, to garnish

### Instructions
Pour the vodka, lime juice, and syrup into an ice-filled Mason jar glass (or another tall glass) in order, finishing up with the soda water or wine. Stir well and garnish with a sprig of rosemary and a lime wedge.

*Rosemary-basil Simple Syrup:* Add 1 sprig of rosemary and 150g (1 cup) of basil leaves to the Simple Syrup recipe (see page 17) while it's still on the heat, once the sugar dissolves.

*Cucumber Vodka:* Peel a large cucumber, cut it in half lengthwise, scoop out the seeds, and chop it into large chunks. Add to clean infusion jar with a lid, cover with 735ml (25fl oz) of vodka, seal, and leave to infuse for 4–7 days.

**79**

# FROZEN MUDSLIDE

The Mudslide is a popular vodka mixed drink made with coffee and Irish cream liqueurs. Similar to the White Russian (see page 28), it's simple and delicious, but it's fun to take that a step further. For the Frozen Mudslide, you'll toss those three original ingredients into the blender with ice and ice cream to create an indulgent boozy milkshake. This drink also deserves to be dressed up with loads of chocolate and whipped cream. There are a few tricks to the chocolate syrup drizzle: work over the sink to prevent spills, hold a previously frozen glass about 15cm (6in) under the syrup bottle and let it slowly drip as you spin and twist the glass, then get it in the freezer right away.

### Ingredients
drizzle of chocolate syrup
30ml (1fl oz) vodka
30ml (1fl oz) coffee liqueur
30ml (1fl oz) Irish cream liqueur
150g (1 cup) vanilla ice cream
whipped cream, grated chocolate, to garnish

### Instructions
Drizzle chocolate syrup inside a chilled hurricane glass (or tall, wide glass) and immediately place it in the freezer. Add the vodka, liqueurs, 150g (1 cup) of crushed ice, and ice cream to the blender and blend until smooth. Pour the mix into the prepared glass and top with a mound of whipped cream and freshly grated chocolate.

FROZEN MUDSLIDE

ORGANIC

COCONUT

WATER

PREMIUM

ANANAS    JOY!

PINEAPPLE

JUICE

100% FRUIT

1L.e

# LIGHT COCONUT MARTINI

Rum is the typical choice for Coconut Martinis, but vodka is an excellent foundation choice as well. This recipe uses Vanilla Vodka (see page 39 for a homemade infusion) for an extra layer of flavour, while a touch of pineapple juice turns the mix into a sort of reversed Piña Colada. Typically made with coconut cream or milk, both the Colada and Coconut Martini tend to be rather thick, but switching to coconut water creates a delightfully light and refreshing cocktail. For the lime juice, you can get away with a squeeze from a wedge – but remember to cut the lime twist before juicing the fruit to reduce waste.

### Ingredients
45ml (1½fl oz) Vanilla Vodka (see page 39)
45ml (1½fl oz) coconut water
30ml (1fl oz) pineapple juice
8ml (¼fl oz) freshly squeezed lime juice
a lime twist, to garnish

### Instructions
Pour all the ingredients into a cocktail shaker, fill it with ice, and shake very well. Strain into a chilled cocktail glass and garnish with a lime twist.

# BLUEBERRY BELLINI

The Bellini was created in the 1940s at Harry's Bar, in Venice, by Giuseppe Cipriani and named after the Italian Renaissance painter, Giovanni Bellini. This sparkling wine cocktail soon reached legendary status. The keys to a spectacular Bellini are a fresh purée of white peaches and Italy's famous prosecco. Peaches and blueberries are a heavenly match. Bringing the two together for a Blueberry Bellini simply requires a quick muddle of blueberries and a shot of Blueberry Vodka.

## Ingredients
4–5 blueberries
60ml (2fl oz) white Peach Purée (see below)
45ml (1½fl oz) Blueberry Vodka (see below)
90–120ml (3–4fl oz) prosecco
a peach slice and a few blueberries, to garnish

## Instructions
In a mixing glass, muddle the blueberries and Peach Purée. Add the Blueberry Vodka and stir well. Fine-strain into a Champagne flute and, pouring very slowly, fill with prosecco, then garnish with the fruit.

**Peach Purée:** Blend 4 medium white peaches (pitted and quartered) with 3 ice cubes, 1 teaspoon fresh lemon juice, and 22ml (¾fl oz) 1:1 Simple Syrup (see page 17), or ½ teaspoon sugar until smooth. Makes 11/2 cups purée; store in the fridge for 1 week.

**Blueberry Vodka:** Add 150g (1 cup) of blueberries to a clean infusion jar with a lid, cover with 735ml (25fl oz) of vodka, seal, and leave to infuse for 5–7 days.

# PEARTINI

When autumn winds blow, turn to the Peartini for a fascinating martini. It features pear-infused vodka (see Christmas Mule, page 120) against a darker background of amaretto and Spiced Simple Syrup. It's probably the most complex syrup you'll make because it requires a handful of warming spices, but it's still easy and the brown sugar creates a deep foundation that's perfect for cold-weather drinks, including coffee, tea, hot cider, or other seasonal cocktails. When juicing the lemon, don't forget to squeeze a bit onto the pear slice to prevent oxidation. Cutting it from the middle of the fruit with the stem intact and laying it in the drink makes an impressive garnish.

### Ingredients
45ml (1 ½fl oz) Pear Vodka (see page 120)
22ml (¾fl oz) amaretto
15ml (½fl oz) Spiced Simple Syrup (see below)
8ml (¼fl oz) fresh lemon juice
a pear slice, to garnish

### Instructions
Shake the Pear Vodka, amaretto, simple syrup, and lemon juice in a shaker with ice and strain into a chilled cocktail glass. Garnish with a pear slice.

*Spiced Simple Syrup:* Bring 240ml (8fl oz) water to a boil with 3 cinnamon sticks, 1 tablespoon orange zest, 1 teaspoon each whole allspice, whole cloves, and grated nutmeg, and ½ vanilla bean split lengthwise. Reduce the heat to a simmer, stir in 150g (1 cup) packed brown sugar until dissolved, remove from the heat, cover, and let cool completely before straining.

# FRENCH MARTINI

A modern classic, the French Martini is an irresistible vodka cocktail that everyone should try at least once. A top-shelf vodka creates a wonderful foundation for the perfect fruit pairing of raspberry and pineapple. Black raspberry liqueurs (Chambord is the most popular option) are very sweet, but the tartness of pineapple offsets that so the martini is not cloying. Drink this one right away to capture the spectacular foam produced by shaken pineapple juice. Even better, use fresh pineapple juice; it's easy if you have an electric juicer, though you can blend or muddle the fruit and strain out the pulp. Generally, 150g (1 cup) of diced pineapple will produce 60ml (2fl oz) of juice, which is more than enough for one drink.

## Ingredients
60ml (2fl oz) vodka
15ml (½fl oz) black raspberry liqueur
45ml (1½fl oz) pineapple juice

## Instructions
Pour the ingredients into a cocktail shaker. Fill with ice, shake well, and strain into a chilled cocktail glass.

# PASSION PEARL COCKTAIL

Vodka is a fantastic companion for other spirits, and the Passion Pearl Cocktail pairs light rum with passion fruit vodka. With the triple sec and lemon juice, it's styled after classic sour drinks, and serving it up gives it a martini vibe. Homemade passion fruit vodka is not the quickest infusion and can take a few weeks. It's a good candidate for a little syrup for a slightly sweeter vodka, and adding lemon slices when it's nearly finished balances out the flavour. Though not too common, commercial passion fruit vodkas are available. Alternatively, make the cocktail with straight vodka and replace all or at least 15ml (½fl oz) of the rum with passion fruit juice. The drink is a little thicker but just as tasty.

### Ingredients
15ml (½fl oz) light rum
45ml (1½fl oz) Passion Fruit Vodka (see below)
15ml (½fl oz) triple sec
15ml (½fl oz) fresh lemon juice
2 dashes of aromatic bitters
a lemon twist, to garnish

### Instructions
Pour the rum, vodka, triple sec, and lemon juice into a cocktail shaker. Fill with ice, shake well, and strain into a chilled cocktail glass. Add the bitters and garnish with a lemon twist.

***Passion Fruit Vodka:*** Scrape the pulp from about 12 passion fruits and add to a clean infusion jar with a lid, cover with 735ml (25fl oz) of vodka, seal, and leave to infuse for 2–3 weeks. Add a few lemon slices during the last week.

# VANILLA ROSE COCKTAIL

If you love floral cocktails and homemade ingredients, the Vanilla Rose Cocktail is an absolute must. It stemmed from a personal passion for herb gardening, and the combination of lavender, rosemary, and vanilla is a delight to the senses. You'll need to make Lavender Simple Syrup and Rosemary Vodka. A muddled vanilla bean gives a sultry base while dry vermouth and lemon juice bring everything into balance.

## Ingredients
½ vanilla bean
15ml (½fl oz) Lavender Simple Syrup (see below)
60ml (2fl oz) Rosemary Vodka (see below)
22ml (¾fl oz) dry vermouth
a splash of freshly squeezed lemon juice
a lemon twist, to garnish

## Instructions
Cut the vanilla bean into a few small pieces and place them in a cocktail shaker with the Lavender Simple Syrup. Muddle well to crush the vanilla. Add the remaining ingredients and fill with ice, then shake very well for about 20 seconds. Fine-strain into a chilled cocktail glass and garnish with a lemon twist.

*Lavender Simple Syrup:* Use 3 tablespoons of lavender buds in the standard Rich Simple Syrup recipe (see page 17), adding the herb after bringing it to a simmer.

*Rosemary Vodka:* Add a 8–10cm (3–4in) sprig of rosemary to a clean infusion jar with a lid, cover with 735ml (25fl oz) of vodka, seal, and leave to infuse for 3–5 days.

# VERY BERRY VODKA MOJITO

Vodka is so versatile that it works well in many cocktails that originally used another type of spirit. Replacing the Mojito's rum with vodka doesn't alter the flavour much, so you still get that cool taste of sparkling lime and mint. Building on that foundation, the Very Berry Vodka Mojito brings in a trifecta of fruits. Fresh blackberrries and a single strawberry are added to the muddle, while raspberry liqueur takes over as the sweetener. Frozen fruit will work, but it needs to be thawed first. The drink can go in several directions as well: add some blueberries, use a fruit, herb, or Vanilla Vodka infusion (see page 39), replace the liqueur with fresh berries and add 2 teaspoons superfine sugar or 15ml (½fl oz) syrup to the muddle, or switch to soda water.

### Ingredients
3 fresh blackberries
1 medium strawberry, sliced
6–8 fresh mint leaves
3 lime wedges
60ml (2fl oz) vodka
15ml (½fl oz) raspberry liqueur
90ml (3fl oz) ginger ale
fresh sprig of mint, some berries, and 1–2 lime slices, to garnish

### Instructions
Muddle the berries, mint, and lime wedges in the bottom of a highball glass until juicy. Add the vodka and raspberry liqueur, stir well to incorporate all the ingredients, and fill the glass with ice cubes. Top with ginger ale and garnish with a sprig of mint, more berries, and a lime slice or two.

# SUMMER SANGRIA

(Serves 4)

Sangria is a wine-based fruit punch with endless possibilities.
While red wine is a good match for the classic choices of
brandy and rum, white wine is a better partner for vodka.
White grape juice adds to the Summer Sangria's light profile
and is backed up by grapes in the fruit medley that includes
pineapple for a tropical taste and raspberries for a pop of
colour. Let the fruits and syrup take care of the sweetness,
and go with a dry white wine like pinot grigio. As with any
sangria, prepare the base a day in advance and store it in
the fridge so the diverse flavours marry and become one. If
you do need it immediately, use chilled wine and soda water.
Frozen grapes are also a great alternative to ice that won't
water it down but help to keep the sangria nice and cold.

### Ingredients
1 bottle of dry white wine
120ml (4fl oz) vodka
240ml (8fl oz) white grape juice
150g (1 cup) seedless grapes
300g (2 cups) cubed pineapple
75g (½ cup) fresh raspberries
120ml (4fl oz) Simple Syrup (see page 17)
480ml (16fl oz) soda water

### Instructions
Combine all of the ingredients except the soda water in
a pitcher. Stir well, cover, and refrigerate overnight (or for
at least 1 hour). Add the soda just before serving over
ice, and ensure each glass gets some of the fruits.

# CIDER DELIGHT

Hard cider is often overlooked as a cocktail ingredient, though it is a nice change of pace from finishing a drink with wine or a mixer. It's also versatile and a good companion to a variety of flavours, including the pomegranate and vodka in the Cider Delight. Homemade Pomegranate Vodka is likely a once-a-year project because it's nearly impossible to find fresh pomegranate outside the winter season. Rather than a single fruit infusion, it's best with the tang of a little lime. Make a few bottles to last a full year or explore commercial options to find your favourite. Elderflower liqueur is available from brands like St-Germain, and homemade elderflower cordial is a good substitute if the flowers grow in your area.

### Ingredients
45ml (1½fl oz) Pomegranate Vodka (see below)
22ml (¾fl oz) elderflower liqueur
15ml (½fl oz) fresh lime juice
8ml (¼fl oz) Simple Syrup (see page 17)
120ml (4fl oz) hard cider
a lime wedge, to garnish

### Instructions
Pour the Pomegranate Vodka, elderflower liqueur, lime juice, and syrup into a cocktail shaker, fill with ice, and shake well. Strain into a double old-fashioned glass over fresh ice, top with hard cider, and garnish with a lime wedge.

***Pomegranate Vodka:*** Gently mash ¾ cup of pomegranate arils and 2 sliced limes in a clean infusion jar with a lid, cover with 735ml (25fl oz) of vodka, seal, and leave to infuse for 5–7 days.

# POMEGRANATE FIZZ

The fizz family of drinks typically uses one of the more flavourful distilled spirits like gin and whisky. However, vodka's adaptability via infusions means it's not out of the running for this classic cocktail style. The Pomegranate Fizz includes Ginger Vodka (see page 55), pomegranate liqueur, and Grapefruit Simple Syrup (see page 40). The three flavours are a natural pairing, and fresh lime juice ties them together. Following fizz cocktail tradition, try this drink with the optional egg white because it creates a luscious foam that's amplified by the soda, and the arils will float on top. When doing so, keep food safety in mind: use only the freshest egg that's been constantly refrigerated, or switch to a pasteurized egg to ensure it's safe to drink.

## Ingredients
60ml (2fl oz) Ginger Vodka (see page 55)
30ml (1fl oz) pomegranate liqueur
15ml (½fl oz) fresh lime juice
15ml (½fl oz) Grapefruit Simple Syrup (see page 40)
1 medium egg white (optional)
60ml (2fl oz) soda water
some pomegranate arils and a lime slice, to garnish

## Instructions
Pour the vodka, pomegranate liqueur, lime juice, Simple Syrup, and egg white into a cocktail shaker. Shake vigorously for 30 seconds, fill the shaker with ice cubes, and shake for another 20–30 seconds. Strain into a tumbler over fresh ice cubes, top up with the soda water, and garnish with a few pomegranate arils and a lime slice.

# PEACH COBBLER

Sweet, creamy, and oh-so-delicious, the Peach Cobbler is
a dessert in a glass. It's a multi-seasonal drink that works
just as well at the peak of the summer's peach season as
it does in autumn and winter, when you want a comforting
cocktail. The homemade peach vodka will last that long,
and this is a great excuse to preserve the fruit's freshness.
With a hazelnut liqueur and cream, the experience is not
complete without the digestive biscuit and brown sugar
rim. You can lighten up the drink by substituting either
milk or half-and-half for the cream, and it should work
equally well with vanilla-flavoured almond or soya milk.

### Ingredients
brown sugar and finely crushed digestive
biscuits, to decorate the glass
30ml (1fl oz) Peach Vodka (see below)
22ml (¾fl oz) hazelnut liqueur
22ml (¾fl oz) heavy cream
a peach slice, to garnish

### Instructions
Combine equal parts of finely crushed digestive biscuits and
brown sugar in a shallow dish. Dip the rim of an old-fashioned
in a second small dish of hazelnut liqueur, then into the sugar
and crushed biscuits to coat the rim (see page 16). Add the
peach vodka, hazelnut liqueur, and cream to a shaker, fill with
ice, and shake very well for about 30 seconds. Strain into the
rimmed glass over fresh ice and garnish with a peach slice.

***Peach Vodka:*** Add 2 or 3 sliced peaches to a clean
infusion jar with a lid, cover with 735ml (25fl oz) of
vodka, seal, and leave to infuse for 5–7 days.

# DAPHNE MARTINI

A quiet summer afternoon led to the development of
this original cocktail in the late 2000s, and it remains a
favourite. The concept is quite simple really: a basic dry
gin martini with Pear Vodka and blue curaçao, yet there's
definitely an allure to enhancing that classic cocktail with
fruity sweetness, and its blue colour is sure to brighten
up any day. To add to its appeal, throw a third fruit
into the mix and drop a few blueberries into the glass.
Like all cocktails that are made entirely of alcohol, be
aware that this is a potent drink – it's why you'll generally
find martinis served at just 90–120ml (3–4fl oz).

### Ingredients
45ml (1½fl oz) gin
45ml (1½fl oz) Pear Vodka (see page 120)
15ml (½fl oz) blue curaçao liqueur
15ml (½fl oz) dry vermouth
a dash of orange bitters
a few fresh blueberries, to garnish (optional)

### Instructions
Pour the ingredients into a cocktail shaker. Fill with
ice, shake vigorously, then strain into a chilled cocktail
glass. If you like, add blueberries to garnish.

# SPIKED CARAMEL LATTE

Vodka isn't typically found in spiked coffee. Straight vodka works if you're just seeking alcohol, but flavoured vodka is required when you want to build an interesting coffee cocktail. The Spiked Caramel Latte uses Vanilla Vodka (see page 39), though caramel vodka is a fun alternative if you have a bottle around. Unlike the coffee-shop drink, there's no need for espresso or foamed milk in this recipe. Instead, brew a strong cup of coffee using your favourite method – pour-over, French press, or stovetop percolator are great options. Cream liqueur (whether Irish cream or something like RumChata) takes over for the latte's milk, while caramel sauce gives it a luscious sweetness. It's also a great iced-coffee cocktail; make cold-brew coffee or chill a hot brew and serve it over ice.

### Ingredients
45ml (1 ½fl oz) Vanilla Vodka (see page 39)
60ml (2fl oz) cream liqueur
2 teaspoons caramel syrup or sauce
150ml (5fl oz) strong-brewed hot coffee
some whipped cream and caramel, to garnish

### Instructions
Pour the vodka, liqueur, and caramel into a coffee glass or mug. Top with hot coffee and stir well. Add a dollop of whipped cream and drizzle with more caramel to serve.

# LAVA FLOW COCKTAIL

(Serves 4)

Popular among Hawaiian tourists, the Lava Flow Cocktail is an eye-catching tropical delight. It's blended in two parts, and the extra work warrants making it for two people. Typically, the bottom layer is made with light and coconut rums, but this version opts for Coconut Vodka (see page 71) alone. It's blended with frozen strawberries to create a fruit-slushy base. To complete the visual effect, the spiked berries are topped with a creamy Piña Colada-like layer of banana, coconut, and pineapple. The recipe's designed for cream of coconut, not coconut cream, which is a key distinction. The former is sold as a drink mixer and has a sweeter taste with a syrupy texture. Coconut cream is unsweetened, thicker, and often paired with syrup when used in drinks.

## Ingredients
90ml (3fl oz) Coconut Vodka (see page 71)
150g (1 cup) frozen strawberries, unthawed
1 large ripe banana, sliced
90ml (3fl oz) cream of coconut
120ml (4fl oz) pineapple juice
300g (2 cups) crushed ice
2 pineapple wedges, to garnish

## Instructions
Blend the vodka and strawberries in a blender until smooth and pour equal amounts into two hurricane glasses or other tall glasses. Rinse the blender and blend the remaining ingredients together until smooth. Slowly pour on top of the strawberry base and garnish each with a pineapple wedge.

ORGANIC
COCONUT
CREAM

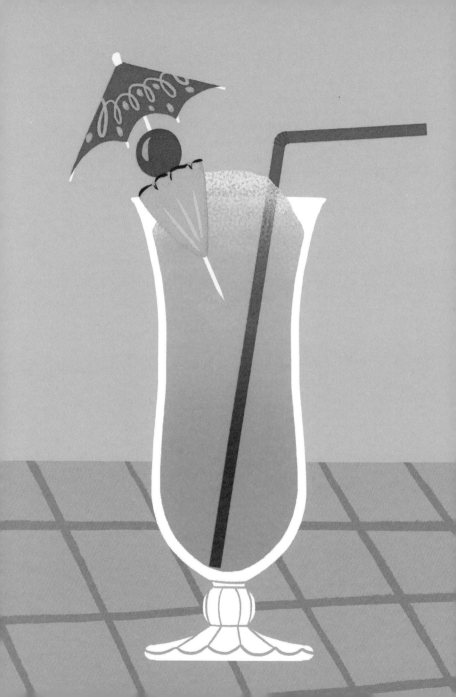

# CHI-CHI

The Chi-Chi is a popular tropical cocktail. While there are
several recipes, pineapple and vodka are the common
factors, and it's most often blended, though sometimes
served on the rocks. Few, however, can outshine the appeal
of this recipe. A lot of its charm comes from the sea-blue
colour – a result of blending blue curaçao with pineapple
– and using ice cream gives it a softer texture than ice
alone. Vodka and cream of coconut are like the backup
singers that ensure a performance goes off without a hitch.
Have fun with tropical fruit infusions in this drink. Almost
any are great alternatives to straight vodka – coconut,
mango, pineapple, and passion fruit are fantastic options.

### Ingredients
60ml (2fl oz) vodka
15ml (½fl oz) blue curaçao liqueur
15ml (½fl oz) cream of coconut
75g (½ cup) cubed pineapple
1 scoop of vanilla ice cream
75g (½ cup) crushed ice
a pineapple wedge and cherry, to garnish

### Instructions
Add all of the ingredients into a blender and blend
until smooth. Pour into a hurricane or margarita glass
and garnish with a pineapple and cherry flag (see
Pineapple Mimosa, page 132).

# GUMMY BEAR MARTINI

When you try to reimagine favourite childhood sweets as an
adult beverage, you get fun cocktails like the Gummy Bear
Martini. The drink itself is a basic combination of Raspberry
Vodka (see below), peach schnapps, and cranberry juice.
It has a sweet-like fruit taste that's enjoyable as is, but this
is one drink that relies entirely on the garnish, which is fun to
nibble on as you sip. Select a rainbow of gummy bears to use
and skewer the little sweets in a row. They can be a bit tough
to pierce without squishing the bear, and a metal cocktail
pick works best; the hole produced by wood skewers may
be too big for the sweet unless it has a really sharp point.

### Ingredients
45ml (1½fl oz) Raspberry Vodka (see below)
30ml (1fl oz) peach schnapps
30ml (1fl oz) cranberry juice
3–5 gummy bears, to garnish

### Instructions
Pour the vodka, peach schnapps, and cranberry juice
into a shaker, fill with ice, shake well, and strain into
a chilled cocktail glass. Add 3–5 gummy bears
onto a cocktail pick and rest the skewer on the rim.

***Raspberry Vodka:*** Add 150g (1 cup) of fresh raspberries to a
clean infusion jar with a lid, cover with 735ml (25fl oz)
of vodka, seal, and leave to infuse for 5–7 days.

•IMPORTED•••

EXTRA SPECIAL

# VODKA

*triple distilled*

40% ALC/VOL

# SAGE AND ROSEMARY BEE'S KNEES

A classic from the days of Prohibition in the USA, the Bee's Knees is a gin cocktail that lives up to its name. Made with nothing more than Honey Syrup and lemon juice, transforming this speakeasy favourite into a vodka cocktail requires a couple of herbs to make up for the lack of gin's botanical flavouring. Sage and rosemary are a great match, and the citrus accents give the drink a delicate vibrancy. This drink is also a good place to use Rosemary Vodka (see page 92).

### Ingredients

3 fresh sage leaves, torn, plus 1 to garnish
1 tablespoon rosemary leaves
22ml (¾fl oz) Honey Syrup (see below)
60ml (2fl oz) vodka
15ml (½fl oz) fresh lemon juice
2 dashes of orange bitters

### Instructions

Muddle the sage, rosemary, and syrup in an old-fashioned glass. Add the vodka and lemon juice, fill with ice, then stir very well for 30 seconds. Finish it with the orange bitters and garnish with a sage leaf.

*Honey Syrup:* Combine 2 parts honey with 1 part water, which helps the thick sweetener dissolve in cold cocktails. Make as much as you like, stirring to an even consistency, and it can be stored in the fridge for up to 2 weeks.

# POMEGRANATE CHAMPAGNE PUNCH

(Serves 16-18)

This Pomegranate Champagne Punch is sure to be a crowd-pleaser. With a combination of pomegranate and cranberry juices backed by Citrus Vodka (see page 27) and Cinnamon Syrup, it's ideal for holiday parties. Switch to plain or another flavoured syrup and it works any time of the year. True Champagne is not necessary and you can save money with another sparkling wine (such as Prosecco); the drier the better to counterbalance the punch's sweetness. Pick a mix of fresh berries, citrus, or other tempting fruits. Large chunks of ice will dilute slowly, and keep your punch cold longer.

### Ingredients
240ml (8fl oz) Citrus Vodka (see page 27)
480ml (16fl oz) pomegranate juice
360ml (12fl oz) cranberry juice
45ml (1½fl oz) fresh lemon juice
45ml (1½fl oz) Cinnamon Simple Syrup (see below)
1 bottle of Champagne
360ml (12fl oz) ginger ale
seasonal fruits and citrus slices, to serve

### Instructions
Place the fruits and some ice in a punch bowl, then add the Citrus Vodka, fruit juices, and syrup. Stir well and add the Champagne and ginger ale just before serving.

***Cinnamon Simple Syrup:*** Add 4 cinnamon sticks and 1/2 teaspoon vanilla extract to the 1:1 Simple Syrup recipe (see page 17).

VERY FANCY
CHAMPAGNE

2008

# AUTUMN SPICED TONIC

A personal infatuation with tonic water and multifaceted vodka infusions led to the development of this seasonal take on the vodka tonic. It begins with a three- to four-day infusion that creates an apple-pear-cinnamon-flavoured vodka, which is then mixed with a splash of Rich Simple Syrup and tonic. The syrup adds a sweetness that marries the drier profile of tonic with the autumn-inspired vodka, though you can skip it if you like. This cocktail is not as transparent as the original vodka drink but has a complexity more like gin and tonic, and it's a brilliant dinner drink for autumn entertaining. Make it as tall or short as you like by simply adding more or less tonic.

### Ingredients
45ml (1½fl oz) Apple-pear-cinnamon Vodka (see below)
a splash of Rich Simple Syrup (see page 17)
90–150ml (3–5fl oz) tonic water, to taste
an apple slice, to garnish

### Instructions
In an ice-filled highball glass, stir together the infused vodka and Simple Syrup. Top up with tonic water to taste and garnish with an apple slice.

*Apple-pear-cinnamon Vodka:* Cut 1 red apple and 1 green or red pear into large pieces, removing any seeds. Add the fruit and 1 cinnamon stick to a clean infusion jar with a lid, cover with 735ml (25fl oz) of vodka, seal, and leave to infuse for 3–4 days.

# CHRISTMAS MULE

While the Moscow Mule is a great year-round drink, when the winter winds begin to blow, it's time for something warm and cosy... enter the Christmas Mule. This recipe was inspired by the original, and features pear-infused vodka. Warming up ginger beer on the hob or in the microwave opens up the mixer's flavour in a surprisingly wonderful way and, if you do so gently enough, a faint hint of the carbonation remains. The taste of ginger beer varies from sweet to extra spicy, and the spicier the better for this drink. Also, don't skip the garnish because the cinnamon stick infuses the drink with its warm spice and marries the pear and ginger flavours in a spectacular way.

## Ingredients
120ml (4fl oz) ginger beer
45ml (1½fl oz) Pear Vodka (see below)
a cinnamon stick, to garnish

## Instructions
Heat the ginger beer for a few minutes in a small saucepan on the hob or for about 10 seconds in the microwave until warmed through. Pour the Pear Vodka into a heatproof glass or coffee mug, then top with the warm ginger beer. Garnish with a cinnamon stick.

**Pear Vodka:** Add 2 sliced pears (1 green and 1 red are really nice) to a clean infusion jar with a lid, cover with 735ml (25fl oz) of vodka, seal, and leave to infuse for 4–5 days.

# SPIKED ARNOLD PALMER

(Serves 4)

To make an Arnold Palmer, all you need is iced tea and lemonade. It's a great foundation for all sorts of additional flavours, and this recipe brings vanilla, blueberry, and peach into the mix. Use black tea for the iced tea, and brew it hot then cool it slowly for the best flavour. For the lemonade, use the basic formula of one part each of sugar and fresh lemon juice with two parts water, then add any more of these three ingredients to adjust it to your taste. Since the drink is all about fresh ingredients, taking the time to make Vanilla Vodka (see Chocolate Martini, page 44) is worth the effort. If you're feeling really crafty, it's easy to find homemade peach liqueur recipes online that can replace the schnapps, too.

## Ingredients
2–3 peaches, sliced
75g (½ cup) blueberries
240ml (8fl oz) Vanilla Vodka (see page 39)
120ml (4fl oz) peach schnapps
720ml (24fl oz) cups iced tea
720ml (24fl oz) fresh lemonade
some peach slices, lemon slices, and blueberries, to garnish

## Instructions
Place the peaches and blueberries in a pitcher, and add the vodka, peach schnapps, iced tea, and lemonade. Stir well and chill until cold or add ice and serve immediately. Pour into ice-filled glasses and garnish with peach and lemon slices and blueberries.

# STRAWBERRY VODKA LEMONADE

(Serves 8-10)

As a refreshing sweet-tart drink, lemonade is an excellent mixer, particularly for vodka and summer fruits. This drink brings those elements together in a pitcher that's great for entertaining or just keeping in the fridge. This is a speedy version that skips making strawberry syrup or lemonade, opting instead for a quick whirl in the blender. Make a full cup of Honey Syrup (see page 115) so you have extra to sweeten the drink as needed. Rather than pouring vodka into the pitcher, keep the base non-alcoholic and add a shot to each glass. The drink also has potential for adaptations; add raspberries or other fruits to the blend, use a flavoured syrup, or make it a sparkling lemonade with a little soda.

## Ingredients

150g (1 cup) sliced, hulled fresh strawberries
120–180ml (4–6fl oz) Honey Syrup (see page 115), to taste
240ml (8fl oz) fresh lemon juice
720ml (24fl oz) water
240ml (8fl oz) Vanilla Vodka (see page 39)
strawberries and lemon slices, to garnish

## Instructions

Blend the strawberries, 120ml (4fl oz) syrup, lemon juice, and water until smooth. Taste and add more syrup to sweeten. Strain through a fine-mesh strainer to remove most of the strawberry seeds, transfer to a pitcher, stir in the vodka, and refrigerate for 1 hour. When ready to serve, stir well, then pour into ice-filled glasses. Add some strawberries and lemon slices to the pitcher or glasses, or both.

SPECIAL
PUMPKIN
VODKA

APPLE
CIDER

# PUMPKIN CIDER

The desire to give everything a pumpkin spin is an annual phenomenon that happens each autumn. In the mid-2000s, pumpkin vodka started trending and several vodka makers released their own version. Many, however, have succumbed to a decreased demand, and it's now almost easier to make it yourself than find a bottle at the off-licence. Since most of the work is put into the vodka, Pumpkin Cider is intentionally kept very simple, adorning that homemade creation with nothing more than apple cider and soda water. It's a satisfying drink that's a refreshing accompaniment to autumn dinner menus.

### Ingredients
45ml (1½fl oz) Pumpkin Vodka (see below)
120ml (4fl oz) apple cider
a splash of soda water
a lemon wedge, to garnish

### Instructions
Pour the Pumpkin Vodka and apple cider into a tumbler filled with ice and top up with a splash of soda water. Garnish with a lemon wedge.

*Pumpkin Vodka:* Coat about 600g (4 cups) of cubed pumpkin in honey and roast in 200°C/400°F oven for 45 minutes. Transfer to a saucepan with 1 or 2 bay leaves, cover with 200ml (6¾fl oz) of water, bring to a boil, mash the pumpkin, then simmer for 1 hour. Remove from the heat, cool, and blend with 300g (2 cups) of vodka, then strain through a cheesecloth-lined fine-mesh strainer. Sweeten with 37.5 to 75g (¼ to ½ cup) Spiced Simple Syrup (see page 87) if desired.

# GARDEN PARTY PUNCH

(Serves 8-10)

Summer affairs are a perfect excuse to showcase the freshest produce of the year, and watermelon is the star of the Garden Party Punch. The fruit is a surprisingly good companion to fresh parsley, and the recipe blends the two ingredients into herb-kissed watermelon juice. The juice needs to be strained very well to remove the pulp and is then ready to be mixed with vodka, lemon juice, and Simple Syrup. Like any sparkling punch, hold the ginger ale until the last minute so guests can enjoy it fully carbonated. Before cutting the melon, consider using it as a punch bowl; cut it about two-thirds from the bottom then scoop out the flesh and pour the punch into the hollow rind.

## Ingredients
1 small watermelon (about 3kg/6-7lb)
37.5g (¼ cup) fresh Italian parsley leaves
360ml (12fl oz) vodka
180ml (6fl oz) fresh lemon juice
180ml (6fl oz) Simple Syrup (see page 17)
720ml (24fl oz) ginger ale
some lemon slices, to garnish

## Instructions
Blend the watermelon and parsley until smooth, then run through a fine-mesh strainer – it should yield about 750g (5 cups) of juice). Add the strained watermelon mix, vodka, lemon juice, and syrup to a pitcher filled with ice. Stir well and chill. Add the ginger ale, then serve over ice and garnish with lemon slices.

# ROSY FRENCH 75

Vanilla is one of the most versatile vodkas you can make
(see page 39). From sweet and creamy to fruity drinks, it
also works well in floral cocktails like the Rosy French 75.
An elegant drink worthy of a spring dinner party or brunch,
this rendition of a classic sparkling wine cocktail relies on
Rose Simple Syrup. It's flavoured with rosewater; look for the
potable variety used for food because some are formulated
for cosmetics and should not be consumed. The syrup is also
sweeter than most to offset the intense floral taste and is
best when made with raw sugar. While you have Rose Simple
Syrup, use it in other transparent cocktails. It's a fantastic
way to sweeten a Vodka Martini and lovely in a Lemon Drop.

### Ingredients
60ml (2fl oz) Vanilla Vodka (see page 39)
1 teaspoon Rose Simple Syrup (see below)
15ml (½fl oz) fresh lemon juice
120ml (4fl oz) prosecco
a lemon twist, to garnish

### Instructions
Pour the vodka, syrup, and lemon juice into a cocktail
shaker, fill with ice, and shake well. Strain into a chilled
Champagne flute that's half-full of ice. Top with
the prosecco and garnish with a lemon twist.

***Rose Simple Syrup:*** Dissolve 300g (2 cups) of raw
sugar in 120ml (4fl oz) of boiling water over a medium
heat, reduce to simmer, add 120ml (4fl oz) of edible
rosewater, cover, and simmer for 15 minutes before
removing from the heat and allowing to cool.

# PINEAPPLE MIMOSA

Double up on the pineapple and give the famous Mimosa a tropical fruit twist. The original bubbly orange juice drink is a great venue for experimentation, and the Pineapple Mimosa will definitely shake up your brunch. With a Pineapple Vodka base, pineapple juice joins the Mimosa's classic ingredients of triple sec and orange juice. Choose your favourite sparkling wine, and don't worry too much about sticking to Champagne; the French wine can be expensive, and budget-friendly options like prosecco or cava are perfect for mixed drinks. This Mimosa is also fabulous with a dry sparkling rosé. For an impressive finishing touch, dress up the drink with a maraschino cherry skewered to a petite pineapple wedge to create a 'flag' garnish.

## Ingredients
30ml (1fl oz) Pineapple Vodka (see below)
15ml (½fl oz) triple sec
15ml (½fl oz) orange juice
15ml (½fl oz) pineapple juice
sparkling wine, to top up
a pineapple wedge and a cherry, to garnish

## Instructions
Into a Champagne flute, pour the vodka, triple sec, and fruit juices. Top up with sparkling wine and garnish with a pineapple wedge and a cherry.

***Pineapple Vodka:*** Add 150g (1 cup) of fresh pineapple chunks to a clean infusion jar with a lid, cover with 735ml (25fl oz) of vodka, seal, and leave to infuse. This infusion takes about 2 weeks because pineapple is such a mild flavour.

# RED PEPPER SPRITZER

Tomato is not the only option for savoury drinks. When a Bloody Mary sounds a bit too heavy, try the Red Pepper Spritzer instead. Though unusual in the drink world, once you get a taste for freshly pressed sweet pepper juice accented with herbs typically reserved for cooking, you'll understand its appeal. The recipe was originally designed as a mocktail, but a little alcohol doesn't hurt the mix, and vodka's neutral flavour is the best choice. If you like, make it with Lemon Vodka (see page 72) and cut the lemon juice in half. This drink is a great way to relish your garden's produce to its fullest and is even more enjoyable when sitting in a sunny garden on a warm day.

### Ingredients
½ medium red bell pepper, seeded and chopped
5 leaves fresh sweet basil
30ml (1fl oz) fresh lemon juice
15ml (½fl oz) Simple Syrup (see page 17)
45ml (1½fl oz) vodka
ginger ale, to top up
a lemon slice, red bell pepper slice,
and thyme sprig, to garnish

### Instructions
Muddle the bell pepper, basil, lemon juice, and syrup in a cocktail shaker to release the pepper's juice. Add the vodka, fill it with ice, and shake vigorously. Fine strain into a double old-fashioned glass over fresh ice, top up with ginger ale, and garnish with lemon and bell pepper slices and a sprig of thyme.

# SNICKERTINI

The Snickertini is guaranteed to satiate your sweet tooth.
A creamy cocktail with the chocolate bar's signature
combination of chocolate and caramel, you'll need
caramel vodka for this recipe. You won't be able to
replicate it at home, though a few vodka brands make it.
As a substitute, use regular or Vanilla Vodka (see page
39) and add a tablespoon or two of caramel syrup.
Chocolate liqueur options are numerous and will alter
the drink in wonderful ways. Go with the sweeter crème
de cacao, a creamier alternative, or seek out unknown
brands that are surprising treats. Rather than the cream,
add an extra splash of Irish cream. Most importantly,
have fun with the chocolate-caramel drizzle. Beyond
looking fabulous, it adds flavour as you drink and is a
fun technique to perfect for any chocolate cocktail.

### Ingredients
45ml (1½fl oz) caramel vodka
15ml (½fl oz) amaretto
15ml (½fl oz) chocolate liqueur
15ml (½fl oz) Irish cream liqueur
a splash of cream
chocolate and caramel sauces, to decorate the glass

### Instructions
First prepare the glass; drizzle chocolate and caramel
sauces inside a frozen cocktail glass (see page 15 for tips)
and place in the freezer while you make the cocktail. Pour
the other ingredients into a cocktail shaker, fill with ice,
and shake until frosty. Strain into the prepared glass.

# KIWI MARTINI

A compelling green martini doesn't have to rely on sweet liqueurs. Instead, turn to the unassuming kiwi fruit. The Kiwi Martini is a simple and unique option when you want something different that's not difficult to make. Once the fuzzy skin is removed, the fruit is easy to juice with a muddler, though you'll definitely want to fine-strain the shaken cocktail to keep most of those tiny seeds out of your glass (inevitably, some will make it through). Pairing kiwi with Honey Syrup (see page 115) and fresh lemon creates a well-balanced vodka martini. For an extra dimension, try it with coconut, passion fruit, or pineapple vodka.

### Ingredients
½ skinned kiwi, sliced, plus 1 slice to garnish
1 teaspoon Honey Syrup (see page 115)
a squeeze of fresh lemon juice
45ml (1½fl oz) vodka

### Instructions
Muddle the kiwi, Honey Syrup, and lemon juice in a cocktail shaker. Add the vodka and some ice, shake well, and fine-strain into a chilled cocktail glass. Garnish with the kiwi slice.

# JALAPEÑO VODKARITA

When the perfect balance of flavours is obtained, spicy cocktails are a thing of wonder. A twist on a very flavourful Margarita, the Jalapeño Vodkarita replaces tequila with vodka. Depending on your affinity for all things hot and spicy, use just a few slices of jalapeño or the entire pepper. Removing the seeds creates a cleaner drink, and the more of the white membrane you cut away, the milder the drink will be because that's where all the capsaicin lies in chillies. Lime juice and the brandy-based orange liqueur Grand Marnier give the cocktail a much-needed tart sweetness that offsets the pepper's heat, while the salted rim adds a brilliant zing to each sip.

## Ingredients
1 jalapeño pepper, seeds removed and sliced
½ teaspoon agave nectar
15ml (½fl oz) fresh lime juice
30ml (1½fl oz) vodka
15ml (½fl oz) Grand Marnier
1 dash of orange bitters
a lime wedge and flaky sea salt, to decorate the glass
a few jalapeño slices, to garnish

## Instructions
Wet the rim of a tumbler with a piece of lime then press the glass into a plate with the flaky sea salt scattered over it (see page 16). In a cocktail shaker, muddle the jalapeño slices, agave nectar, and lime juice. Add the spirits and bitters, fill with ice, and shake well. Strain into the prepared glass over fresh ice and garnish with a few extra jalapeño slices.

**140**

# INDEX

# CREDITS

**Colleen Graham would like to thank:**
As always, my foremost gratitude must go to my husband, Shannon.
He is tremendously supportive behind the scenes and always willing
to test recipes during development. To family, friends, and colleagues
who have helped in this journey, a big thank you as well!

I could not dive deep into this subject without the collective knowledge
of the cocktail and food community. There are far too many people to
mention from whom I've learned over the years, and every one of them
has contributed their own specialties to aid all of us in understanding
what it takes to make great drinks. I'm sure we'll all keep doing our part!

Finally, there are two invaluable resources that I highly recommend to anyone
who wants to really study drinks. *The Flavor Bible*, by Karen Page and Andrew
Dornenburg, is a constant reference for creative flavor pairings and rarely
leaves my desk. A new addition to the library, *The Oxford Companion to Spirits
and Cocktails*, edited by David Wondrich and Noah Rothbaum, is beyond
valuable. I was one of those kids who randomly read the encyclopedia, and
I find myself doing the same with this hefty volume because it's fascinating.

**Ruby Taylor would like to thank:**
Eddie and Lucy.